FINN'S FUN
ACTIVITY BOOK

PUFFIN BOOKS

UK | USA | Canada | Ireland | Australia
India | New Zealand | South Africa

Puffin Books is part of the Penguin Random House group of companies whose addresses can be found at
global.penguinrandomhouse.com.

puffinbooks.com

This edition first published 2016
Content first published 2015
001

Written by Kirsten Mayer
Illustrations by Patrick Spaziante and Stephen Reed
Text and illustrations copyright ©Cartoon Network, 2016
ADVENTURE TIME, CARTOON NETWORK, the logos, and all related characters and elements
are trademarks of and © Cartoon Network. (s15)

The National Literacy Trust is a registered charity no: 1116260 and a company limited by guarantee no. 5836486
registered in England and Wales and a registered charity in Scotland no. SC042944. Registered address: 68 South
Lambeth Road, London SW8 1RL.
National Literacy Trust logo and reading tips © National Literacy Trust 2016
www.literacytrust.org.uk/donate

Set in Pendlefont
Printed in Great Britain

A CIP catalogue record for this book is available from the British Library

ISBN: 978-0-141-37072-9

www.greenpenguin.co.uk

WELCOME
to the
LAND of OOO

PUFFIN

This book belongs to someone who is
rad, fast, and adequate.
Their name is:

_____

Who did this?!
The answer is at the
back of this book . . .

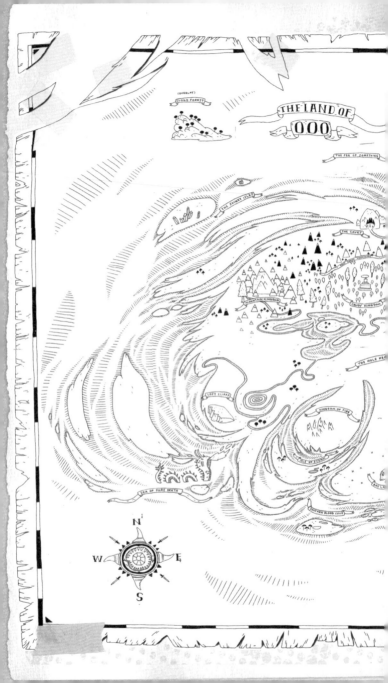

WELCOME to the

GRASS LANDS

Finn and Jake live in an awesome Tree Fort. There are secret rooms, a Treasure Room, a Weapon Room, and two Living Rooms!

ROOF FOR STARGAZING AND PARTIES

FINN AND JAKE'S ROOM

LIVING ROOM 2

LIVING ROOM

ATTIC

WEAPON ROOM

HOLLOW TRUNK

TREASURE ROOM

YARD

YURT

11

What if you lived in a tree? Use these pages to design your own Tree Fort. What secret rooms would you have? How would you get around? Would you use ladders or ropes?

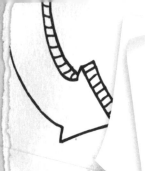

Finn likes to draw
with both his left
and right hands —
at the same time.
Test your skills!

Draw with
your left hand
on this page.

14

Draw at the same time!

Draw with your right hand on this page.

ADVENTURE TIME!

Oh no! The **HOT DOG** Princess is in trouble! Finn uses his **SPAGHETTI LIMBS** to distract the **ICE KING**, while Jake gives advice about **DRINKING WATER**. Suddenly, **BMO** swoops in to save the day!

Fill in the blanks to write your own
rescue adventures for Finn and Jake.

Oh no! The _____ Princess is in trouble!
Finn uses his _____ to distract the
_____,
while Jake gives advice about _____.
Suddenly, _____ swoops in to save the day!

Oh no! The _____ Princess is in trouble!
Finn uses his _____ to distract the
_____,
while Jake gives advice about _____.
Suddenly, _____ swoops in to save the day!

Oh no! The _____ Princess is in trouble!
Finn uses his _____ to distract the
_____,
while Jake gives advice about _____.
Suddenly, _____ swoops in to save the day!

DEAR Begs the Question

Jake writes an advice column every week called Begs the Question. Squirrel always sends in letters — but they never get printed!

Dear Begs the Question,
My friend stole my favourite video game, and now I never see him because he's playing it all the time.
—Empty House

Example

Dear Empty House,
Eat breakfast because you need your protein. Then go to your friend's house, hook up your controller, and play the video game with him all day long. Drink eight glasses of water while playing. And don't forget to wear pants.
—Begs the Question

On this page, write some questions for Jake. Then, write some advice.

Dear Begs the Question,

_____

_____

_____

_____

_____

_____

Answer:

_____

_____

_____

_____

_____

_____

_____

ROCKIN' LYRICS

Keep a journal like Marceline did to inspire your song lyrics. Write some journal entries on these pages. Wait a week, then come back and highlight some good stuff for your tunes.

_____

_____

_____

_____

_____

_____

_____

_____

_____

_____

_____

_____

Jake can get
stretchy with it!
He stretches out to
form another shape.
Draw it here.

Cool, dude!

The goblins always have a king to rule them. When Finn and Jake first met them Xergiok was king. Then, some stuff happened, Finn used his sword and he became King of the Goblins.

Finn's gonna need a queen. I'll do it.

Finn and Jake didn't like following the Goblin rules, so they left Whisper Dan on the throne and sneaked out.

A line of succession is the list of rulers for a kingdom in the order they ruled. The line of succession for the Goblin Kingdom is:

If you ruled a kingdom, who would you want to rule after you? Fill out your own line of succession.

Xergiok

Finn

Whisper Dan

Here's what the Goblin King throne looks like:

Now, design your own throne here!

The Goblin Palace is pretty awesome.
It has a throne room, Goblin birthing pits,
dragon stables, a royal video-game room and
a royal bedroom with optional bunk beds!

If you were the Goblin King, what would your palace look like? Draw your floor plans and room designs here!

HOT LAVA!

The Fire Kingdom is a dangerous place, full of volcanoes and hot lava. Draw a path to safety through the burning stuff!

Start
here

You're safe!

Solve these mazes! But don't just solve them — collect as many princesses as you can along the way. Then bring them to the Ice King, so he can MARRY THEM!

LEVEL 1

Start

End

Congratulations! You solved Level 1!
Now go on to Level 2!

LEVEL 2

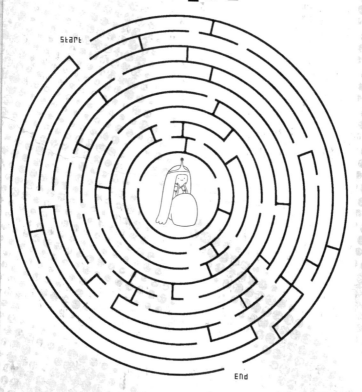

start

End

Congratulations! You solved Level 2!
Now go on to Level 3!

LEVEL 3

Start

End

Almost there! You solved Level 3!
Now go on to the final level!

FINAL LEVEL

USE a PEN . . . iF YOU DARE! HAHAHA!

End

Colour-me-in Gunters

Lock up the Ice King by drawing
more bars on his prison cell.

These bars won't
hold me forever . . .
There's only, like,
two of them!

WIZARD

The Rules:

Contestants will fight each other with spells from the eight schools of magic.

No science!

No weapons!

You must be a wizard.

No one is allowed to exit a Wizard Battle. If you quit, you will be turned into a cat.

Here's a list of Wizard Battle competitors:

Ice King	Dimension Wizard
Rock Wizard	Flame Lord
Naked Wizard	Laser Wizard
Huntress Wizard	Abracadaniel

BATTLE!

Here's a list of wizard powers:

Ice Power — can freeze things

Rock Power — can summon a meteor shower

Storm Power — a magic staff can summon storms

Hunting Power — fires magic arrows

Dimension Power — opens a portal through which a centipede appears

Fire Power — creates flames

Laser Power — shoots lasers

Rainbow Power — it can turn people into different colours

Set up your own Wizard Battle! Choose the competitors to do battle and the powers they will battle with. Then decide who wins and moves on to the next round until you have one final champion!

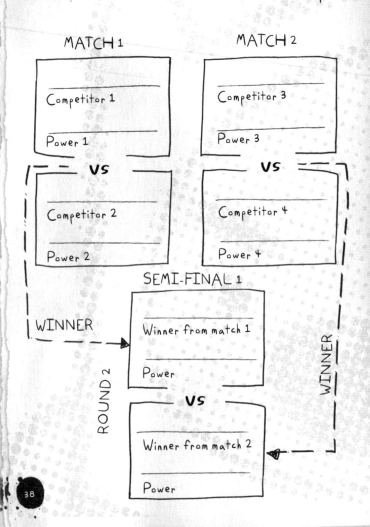

MATCH 1

Competitor 1

Power 1

VS

Competitor 2

Power 2

MATCH 2

Competitor 3

Power 3

VS

Competitor 4

Power 4

WINNER

SEMI-FINAL 1

Winner from match 1

Power

VS

Winner from match 2

Power

ROUND 2

WINNER

By the rays of the setting sun, the battle of wizards has begun!

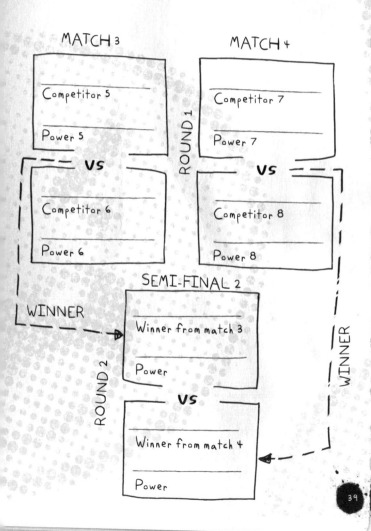

MATCH 3

Competitor 5

Power 5

VS

Competitor 6

Power 6

MATCH 4

Competitor 7

Power 7

VS

Competitor 8

Power 8

ROUND 1

WINNER

SEMI-FINAL 2

Winner from match 3

Power

VS

Winner from match 4

Power

ROUND 2

WINNER

FINAL WIZARD BATTLE

Semi-final 1 winner
_____

Power

VS.

Semi-final 2 winner
_____

Power

JOIN THE WIZARD SECRET SOCIETY

Some wizards are in a secret group where they get together and do secret wizardy things. They have a secret hand signal (they make a W with their fingers) and a secret oath:

In shadow, we find the light,
Safety sealed in darkest night.
So make sure y'all keep it tight.
Wizards only, fools!

Make up your own secret society,

and invite your friends to join!

Name: _____

Members: _____

_____

_____

_____

Secret hand signal:
(draw it here)

Secret oath: _____

_____

_____

_____

_____

_____

43

Tell the Future

The Cosmic Owl appears to Finn in dreams and tells him what's going to happen in the future. If you could find out the future in a dream, what would you want to know about?

Write about a dream that shows a future you would like to see:

_____

_____

_____

_____

_____

_____

_____

_____

_____

_____

Last night I dreamt about:

Five Short Graybles Word Search

Find all of these words in the word search below!
The words could be across, down or diagonal.

Cuber   Taste   Gunter   Talent Show
Theme   Sandwich   Armpits   Basketball
Touch   Jellyfish   Sound   Grocery Kingdom
Smell   Bread   Grayble

```
D T U Z P S T R D D A E R B G
E G N Z C A T O P U L F A V R
A U V C S P G I W F D J L K O
N N M T Z Z X L P S R D L B C
C T E K P M I E E M Y J A I E
L E G R A Y B L E U R B B P R
B R N A X B U N O U L A T S Y
T J E L L Y F I S H Q Z E D K
G S W O H S T N E L A T K N I
I D H X C U B E R S Z P S U N
J R R S R T O U C H I P A O G
W G X K L L E M S L E P B S D
R S H C I W D N A S Z F I G O
R T K G U L M K O Q W M T C M
Y L X T H E M E Q H R X S K Q
```

Five More Graybles
Word Search

Now find all of *these* words
in the word search below!

Lady Rainicorn   Tree Trunks   Tea   Bitter
    Sweet   Sour   Fingers   Football
   Savoury   Shelby   Bride
  Wizard Bill   Salty   Ring

```
E I W R T E E W S G Y K Z T
L O I M R S A H C U E Z R E
J X Z G U I B N G J K E L L
O C A V A T N W W M E K D E
T F R G B I T G Y T S X K A
C O D J G E S W R T I V F Q
A O B C A F Y U T K L I L D
X T I P Q R N V J F K A S F
Z B L D U K D S S Z T S S A
N A L W S E F I N G E R S X
Y L N P I Y B L E H S P B S
T L R E T T I B I C B K X O
T E D I R B Y R U O V A S U
L A D Y R A I N I C O R N R
```

Oh my glob, Lumpy Space Princess is totally in need of a lumpin' new crown to wear! She is a princess, after all. Design her some new ones to choose from here.

Promcoming is a totally HUGE deal in Lumpy Space.

Who would you want to go to Promcoming with?

_____

_____

How would you want to arrive?
☐ Cloud car
☐ Limo
☐ Riding on a Rainicorn

If you were going to the dance with LSP and Melissa, what would you wear? Design your Promcoming outfit here:

Don't forget
your shoes!
Draw some here:

Be Honest.

OR ELSE.

Flame Princess prefers people to be honest with her above all else — she had a hard time forgiving Finn for betraying her. Give honest answers to these questions or Flame Princess will kick you out of the kingdom!

What's your favourite colour?

_____

_____

_____

_____

_____

_____

_____

What colour are your underpants?

Who is your best friend?

Who do you tell everyone
is your best friend?

Prized Possessions

Flame Princess sends Finn and Jake into the dangerous Fire Kingdom to get her scented candles — that's a big favour! What items do you own that you can't live without? If your house was on fire which things would you want to save?

I feel sad. I left all my scented candles at the castle. It's OK, though, because Finn and Jake are gonna get them for me!

List them here!

You may have noticed that Flame Princess has a short temper! Do you? Write down things that make you mad on this page.

_____

_____

_____

_____

_____

_____

Next time one of these things makes you want to blow your top, write about it here until you're not mad any more.

_____

_____

_____

_____

_____

_____

Uh oh! Flame Princess is mad! Fill these pages with flames of rage and colour them in with reds, oranges and yellows!

ANSWERS

HOT LAVA!
Pages 28-29

Start here

You're safe!

Page 30

start

End

Page 31

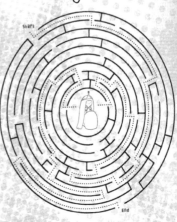

start

End

Page 32

Start

Page 33

Start

End

Five Short Graybles
Word Search — page 46

```
D T U Z P S T R D D A E R B G
E G N Z C A T O P U L F A V R
A U V C S P G I W F D J L K O
N N M T Z Z X L P S R D L B C
C T E K P M I E E M Y J A I E
L E G R A Y B L E U R B B P R
B R N A X B U N O U L A T S Y
T J E L L Y F I S H Q Z E D K
G S W O H S T N E L A T K N I
I D H X C U B E R S Z P S U M
J R R S R T O U C H I P A O G
W G X K L L E M S L E P B S D
R S H C I W D N A S Z F I G O
R T K G U L M K O Q W M T C M
Y L X T H E M E Q H R X S K Q
```

Five More Graybles
Word Search — page 47

```
E I W R T E E W S G Y K Z T
L O I M R S A H C U E Z R E
J X Z G U I B N G J K E L L
O C A V A T N W W M E K D E
T F R G B I T G Y T S X K A
C O D J G E S W R T I V F Q
A O B C A F Y U T K L I L D
X T I P Q R N V J F K A S F
Z B L D U K D S S Z T S S A
N A L W S E F I N G E R S S
Y L N P I Y B L E H S P B S
T L R E T T I B I C B K X O
T E D I R B Y R U O V A S U
L A D Y R A I N I C O R N R
```

End

61

Did you guess
who the culprit is?

It's Jake!

Reading Tips

The **National Literacy Trust** is a charity that transforms lives through literacy. We want to get more families reading. Reading is fun and children who read in their own time do better at school and later in life. By partnering with McDonald's, we hope to encourage more families to read together.

Here are some of our top tips for reading with children.

A good way to bring a book to life is to put on different voices for different characters in the story.

Why not stop at certain points in the story to ask your child what *they* think will happen next?

Setting aside some time to read with your child every day is something both of you can look forward to.

A shared love of reading can last a lifetime. You can still read aloud to your child, even when they are confident enough to read by themselves.

If your child is excited by the subject of a story, it will help keep their interest as you read together, so help them choose the books you'll read together.